Reading

DEVELOPING ADULT TEACHING AND LEARNING: PRACTITIONER GUIDES

Maxine Burton

promoting adult learning

(England and Wales)
21 De Montfort Street
Leicester LE1 7GE

Company registration no. 2603322
Charity registration no. 1002775
Published by NIACE in association with NRDC.

NIACE has a broad remit to promote lifelong learning opportunities for adults.
NIACE works to develop increased participation in education and training,
particularly for those who do not have easy access because of class, gender, age,
race, language and culture, learning difficulties or disabilities, or insufficient
financial resources.

For a full catalogue of all NIACE's publications visit
www.niace.org.uk/publications

Cataloguing in Publications Data
A CIP record for this title is available from the British Library
ISBN 978-1-86201-339-1

Cover design by Creative by Design Limited, Paisley
Designed and typeset by Creative by Design Limited, Paisley
Printed and bound by Aspect Binders and Print Ltd

Developing adult teaching and learning: Practitioner guides

This is one of several linked publications arising from the five Effective Practice Studies carried out by the National Research and Development Centre for Adult Literacy and Numeracy (NRDC) from 2003 to 2007.

The five studies explored effective teaching and learning in reading, writing, numeracy, ESOL and using ICT. To date, three series of publications have been produced from the Effective Practice Studies: the research reports and the development project reports, all published by NRDC; and these practitioner guides, published in partnership between NIACE and NRDC.

For more information on the first two series, please see **www.nrdc.org.uk**

Contents

Acknowledgements

The author would like to thank the following people for their contribution to this publication:

Members of the Consultation Group

(Those indicated by * also worked as practitioner-researchers on the Reading Study and by + also took part in the Oral Reading Fluency Development Project)

- Colette Beazley *
- Judy Davey *
- Richard Finnigan *
- Gill Fuller *
- Liz Heydon *
- Naomi Horrocks*
- Gaye Houghton *
- Hugo Kerr
- Jill Reilly
- Jan Wainwright *+
- Janet Whitfield

The above group of practitioners ('consultant teachers'), some of whom are also teacher-trainers, researchers and managers, were responsible for many of the insights, quotes and examples in the publication, and took an active role throughout the writing of it.

Advisers

Greg Brooks and Pam Cole, both from the University of Sheffield.

Peer review

This guide was peer reviewed. The critical readers were:

- Cynthia Klein
- Yvonne Spare
- Helen Sunderland

About this guide

This guide arose from the findings of a major research project on the teaching of reading in adult literacy classrooms (the 'research study'). In close consultation with a group of 11 experienced practitioners, teacher-trainers and managers, plus a further action research group of teachers (trialling oral reading fluency), we have extended the original research findings to include other helpful guidelines for teaching reading to adults. The findings from the research study are described in Section 2, guidelines from other research are discussed in Section 3 and Section 4 draws on practitioners' experience and insights.

It is not intended to be a comprehensive guide on how to teach reading, although it is very much informed by what happens in today's adult literacy classrooms and by the concerns of today's teachers – and where we can, we use the actual words of both teachers and learners. It does not cover all aspects of teaching reading and, although relevant to many teaching contexts, does not seek to explore issues around assessment, embedded learning, dyslexia and other learning disabilities, or multilingual classrooms. About a fifth of learners in the research study were said to have dyslexia, and around a tenth had a first language other than English; however we found that neither factor seemed to have an impact on their achievement. There is a parallel guide in this series for teachers working with ESOL learners.

We hope the guide will be used as a source of ideas and suggestions for classroom practice, and in each section we provide suggestions for further reading. Above all we hope it will help to stimulate reflection by teachers on their own practice.

Introduction

Setting the scene

The starting point for this guide is the large-scale Study on Effective Practice in the Teaching of Reading to Adult Learners 2003–06 (the 'research study'). This is the largest study in Britain to date of the strategies used to teach reading in adult literacy classes. In the following chapters we look in some detail at what we found – and didn't find – and what this means for practice and professional development. As well as relating the findings to the wider literature on adult literacy, we also include insights on the whole area of teaching reading from our consultation group and other practitioners ('professional wisdom').

Before we do this, we will consider briefly what we mean by 'reading'.

What is reading? Some theories

Three main theoretical approaches to literacy have been identified.

Literacy is a set of neutral *skills* of increasing difficulty to be gradually acquired (usually in school) at certain stages of a person's individual development; when acquired these skills can be applied and used in any context.

The *social practice* approach places the key focus on the various contexts (including the school context) in which literacy and its associated activities are learned. The assumption is that literacy cannot escape the influences of the social, cultural and political contexts which generate it, and that individuals always acquire literacy as part of a social activity.

Literacy is not only a social practice but also a '*critical*' process; literacy and its acquisition are seen as a way of *transforming* people's lives by making people aware of the state in which they exist, with literacy as a means of liberation and empowerment.

A significant reason for rejecting reading as simply a mechanical process is the awareness that it is entrenched in emotions and values. Research (e.g. Chapman and Tunmer, 2003; Galbraith and Alexander, 2005) clearly demonstrates how a spiral of failure and deadened aspiration soon forms if emergent readers are not handled appropriately.

There was an ingrained belief by the learners that they could not read and they could do nothing about it. They firmly believed that external influences controlled what they could and couldn't achieve. (Consultant teacher)

It may well be the case that reading difficulties are felt to be even more embarrassing than problems with writing. It is generally accepted that learners' writing ability often lags behind their reading. When we debated why we saw so few classes advertised as offering just 'reading', it was suggested that learners don't want to admit they need help with reading – 'reading goes to the soul' (consultant teacher). But another consultant teacher was able to give examples of learners (around E1) who were 'happy' to read in her 'reading' class.

To separate the teaching of reading and writing is often regarded as contentious (Street, 2005). Although this guide focuses on reading and there is a parallel guide on writing, this should not be taken to imply an endorsement of separation, merely a recognition that there is value in considering the skills and strategies separately. In practice, integrating both is helpful. And a further consideration is funding, whereby it may be perceived as easier to meet targets by offering 'literacy' provision rather than just 'reading'.

How helpful do you feel it is to make a distinction between reading and writing in planning your teaching?

It is outside the scope of this guide to examine the value-laden context of literacy and associated stigma, and engage fully with the different and sometimes contentious narratives about literacy. There is much stimulating writing out there on these approaches, and suggestions for further reading are included at the end of this section. However an important point needs to be made; these narratives need not be regarded as mutually exclusive, and the skills-based focus of this publication does not deny the validity of other approaches. It will always remain good practice for literacy skills to be related to a context relevant to the learner and to be presented in a way that is supportive of the learner's needs.

So what is reading then?

A starting point might be 'creating or deriving meaning from text' – which was the definition used in the research study. Comprehension is the main point of reading which involves mastery of a complex system of interrelated skills. The traditional division into text, sentence and word (as in the *Adult Literacy Core Curriculum*) recognises that the skills operate on different levels. Although this suggests a hierarchy of complexity, in practice, the three levels need to be taught together.

Much has been written about what goes on in the reading process at the level of initial literacy (e.g. Adams, 1994). Section 3 of Good and Holmes (1978) has some helpful pointers for adults, as has Chapter 2 ('Understanding reading instruction for adult learners') of an American manual by Susan McShane (2005). She lists six requirements for reading:

- An understanding of how speech sounds are related to print
- Decoding (word-identification) skills
- Fluency
- Vocabulary and background knowledge
- Active comprehension strategies
- A motivation to read

The full text of this can be downloaded from
**http://www.nifl.gov/partnershipforreading/publications/html/mcshane/
chapter2.html**

If you want to find out more

The research study

Brooks, G., Burton, M., Cole, P. and Szczerbiński, M. (2007) *Effective Teaching and Learning: Reading.* London: NRDC.

Theories and contexts of literacy

Barton, D. (1994) *Literacy.* Oxford: Blackwell.

Barton, D. and Hamilton, M. (1998) *Local Literacies.* London: Routledge.

Holme, R. (2004) *Literacy: An Introduction*. Edinburgh University Press. (An up-to-date textbook on literacy, recommended by one of the consultant teachers.)

Mace. J. (1995) *Literacy, Language and Community Publishing: Essays in Adult Education*. Clevedon: Multilingual Matters.

Street, B. (1984) *Literacy in Theory and Practice*. Cambridge University Press.

Street, B. (2005) 'Understanding and defining literacy'. Paper commissioned for the *Education for All Global Monitoring Report 2006, Literacy for Life*.

Stubbs, M. (1981) *Language and Literacy*. London: Routledge & Kegan Paul. ('Old, but very enlightening and thought-provoking on the subject of what the English language really is.')

The reading process from an adult perspective

Good, M. and Holmes, J. (1982) *How's it going? An Alternative to Testing Students in Adult Literacy*. ALBSU.

McShane, S. (2005) *Applying Research in Reading Instruction for Adults. First Steps for Teachers*. Washington, DC: National Institute for Literacy. (Can be downloaded from **http://www.nifl.gov/partnershipforreading/publications/html/ mcshane** from which there are links to all the chapters. Useful American work.)

1 What does the research study tell us about the teaching and learning of reading?

Factors that affect progress

We found out a lot about the learners themselves as well as what went on in adult literacy classrooms. Some factors that seemed to affect progress are totally outside the control of teachers, although awareness of them could be helpful.

Factors outside teachers' control

■ **Gender**

Women made slightly better progress than men. It is not clear whether the fact that the majority of practitioners are women has any bearing on this.

■ **Occupational status**

Employed people made better progress than the unemployed. Here there may be issues of learners' motivation, confidence and literacy needs.

■ **Qualifications**

People with formal qualifications (FE/NVQ) made better progress than those with no qualifications. Again, confidence and habits of learning may be involved.

Factors which can be influenced by practitioners
Regular attendance

Learners who attended regularly made better progress.

The benefits of regular attendance were also found by the 1998–99 Basic Skills Agency study of adult learners' progress in literacy (Brooks *et al.*, 2001).

There are, of course, classes where attendance is non-voluntary, e.g. is made a condition of receiving benefits (and for implications of this, see O'Grady and Atkin, 2005/6). But where no such coercion applies, practitioners do tend to be very understanding of and make allowances for some learners' poor attendance and unpunctuality. Certainly there are instances where shift work or family responsibilities can make regular attendance difficult. However, teachers need to be wary of falling into the trap of treating learners too cautiously – 'with kid

"**Learners who attended regularly made better progress**"

gloves', as one of our practitioner group described it – and thereby actually undermining learners' powers of assuming responsibility for their own learning. Establishing a pattern of attendance is important, and contact can be maintained, e.g. by telephone, with learners who 'disappear' to encourage them to return; again sensitivity is important to avoid any appearance of 'hassling' but the longer a learner is absent, the harder it is for him/her to feel comfortable about returning.

Self-study

Learners who reported they had spent more time studying at home between classes made better progress

"Learners who reported they had spent more time studying at home between classes made better progress"

This is another finding that is backed up by other research, a US study (Reder, 2005). Teachers can give various reasons for a reluctance to set 'homework' – because of the school connotations, or concern that learners will be too scared or embarrassed to return to class because they have not completed homework. However, self-study can significantly increase the amount of learning time/exposure to reading.

There is, of course, more to homework than worksheets: the aim should be to find work that empowers learners and that relates to a context which is relevant for them.

Homework ideas

Reading along with audio tapes.

- **Taking photographs of signs to reinforce social sight vocabulary.**
- **A webquest.**
- **Looking out for articles or adverts in local newspapers.**
- **Simply asking your learners to make a note of how many pages of a book they manage to read at home each day.**

A practitioner who regularly sets homework justifies it as follows:

I like homework. This is because I think two hours a week is too little time to understand, retain, own and autonomously deploy learned stuff...I have not had many students disagreeing with the proposal that two hours a week is seriously minimal, nor failing to do their homework as suggested (Consultant teacher)

Homework, like classroom work, should be discussed and negotiated with your learners. And remember that not all learners may have a quiet place at home suitable for study; other venues, such as the local or college library, can be suggested.

Another imaginative approach to increasing opportunities for study time is to link work in the classroom with a group activity outside: for an account of the study of a book/play (Daphne du Maurier's *Jamaica Inn*) and associated materials, followed up by a theatre trip, see an article by Trish Cooney (2005). Indeed practice in play reading by learners (*To Kill a Mockingbird*) was linked very effectively with a prior theatre visit (see 'Oral reading fluency', p. 7). And learners rehearsing a play could perhaps arrange to meet to practise during a holiday/half-term break.

If you do not regularly set homework, list your reasons for not doing so. Do you think your learners would agree with these reasons? And whether you usually offer homework or not, think about imaginative ways you could involve your learners in creating extra opportunities for study.

Time to learn

Learners need enough time to learn.

Opportunities for study are vital. This emerged very strongly in the research study. The average amount of class attendance between the first and the last reading assessments was only about 30 hours and, overall, there was little improvement in the learners' scores. Research from the USA and England suggests that learners require at the very least 150 hours of study ('time on task', which can include time spent learning outside, as well as inside, the classroom) if they are to progress by one level within the *Skills for Life* qualifications framework.

"Learners need enough time to learn"

Self-esteem and confidence

One rather surprising finding from the research study was around the issue of learners' self-esteem and confidence. We found that learners' self-confidence improved during the time they attended classes, and this is usually regarded as essential if learners are to make progress. However, we found no correlation between their increase in confidence and improvement in reading. It seems that its relationship with making measurable progress is much more complex than simple 'cause and effect'.

Increase in learners' self-confidence is always valued by teachers. Think through the reasons for this and see how it might relate to progress in learning.

What did we learn from the classroom practice that we observed?

Two important things emerged:

Learners who spent more time working in pairs made better progress.

"Learners who spent more time working in pairs made better progress"

The advantage of this strategy is that learners work with greater independence than in a one-to-one situation with the teacher/assistant but at the same time there is a less intensive use of the teacher's time. It can work with mixed ability classes, either with learners at similar levels being paired, or with a more able learner helping a less able learner. (There are still benefits for the more able partner in that confidence can be increased, and knowledge consolidated. Teaching is often the best way of really learning something.)

Sometimes learner pairs form spontaneously within a class, sometimes they can be incorporated into the lesson plan, using, for example, paired reading or reciprocal teaching (see 'Oral reading fluency', p. 7 and 'Reciprocal teaching', p. 11). And sometimes there can be resistance to suggested pairings. Above all the teacher will need to be responsive to the social dynamic within a class and remain flexible. The following vignette illustrates this, showing how the teacher 'seized the moment' to provide a buddying opportunity.

Following on from a lesson on pronouns, teacher A distributes a set of photocopied articles from the local newspaper for her class to read and then to pick out the pronouns from. She tells the five learners to get highlighter pens and 'choose the article you want to read. You can work in pairs.' Two learners start reading together but the rest work independently on their chosen articles. A sixth learner, J, then arrives late. A tells her that learner S will explain what she has to do (laughter from S – 'if I can!'). S explains the task accurately to J but even they do not then continue to work together as a pair. At no stage does A attempt to intervene in the learners' preferred groupings. (From the research study)

Think about the above scenario. Do you think the teacher should have insisted they work in pairs? Is there any way she might have encouraged them to work in pairs?

Learners who spent less time working alone in class made better progress.

Working alone is best regarded as 'practising' time and used for limited periods of class time. Quiet time is still necessary for reflection and in order to consolidate learning, and too noisy an environment limits concentration. But time spent this way is obviously at the expense of more 'active' tuition. A common scenario in the adult literacy classroom is learners working individually, with the teacher moving around and 'checking in' with each in turn. One danger of this approach, as we saw in the research study, is learner dependency, if they are left to wait passively for an inappropriate length of time for feedback and/or new work to be given to them.

The *Adult Literacy Core Curriculum* has encouraged more whole-class teaching. Certainly overall the two commonest groupings we saw were whole-class teaching and individual work, which often appeared in a 'groupwork followed by practice' model, typically an opening whole-class session with individual, differentiated work afterwards. (For those of you wondering why one-to-one teaching didn't feature strongly, we were not looking at 'drop-in' type classes where one-to-one tuition is the norm.)

Although there are clear messages about classroom grouping issues from the research study, there was less helpful information about effective strategies for teaching reading. Silent reading was the 'activity' that happened most often, corresponding with the large amounts of time learners spent working alone. 'Active' reading tuition (as opposed to reading silently or doing worksheets) took up less than half the class time, although in fairness, most classes offered general 'literacy' rather than just 'reading'. However, there were several approaches to teaching reading which research suggests are effective but were hardly seen. We shall explore these in Section 3.

By way of summary,

> *One of the most important things to help learners make progress seems to be finding ways of expanding the time they can spend 'on task', both inside and outside the classroom.*

"Learners who spent less time working alone in class made better progress"

"One of the most important things to help learners make progress seems to be finding ways of expanding the time they can spend 'on task', both inside and outside the classroom"

Expanding time spent 'on task' inside and outside the classroom is crucial to helping learners make progress, especially since provision typically takes the form of just one class a week.

Teachers can try to:

- show they value regular attendance by encouraging learners to take responsibility for their own learning;

- encourage learners to do homework and other related activities;

- limit the time spent in the classroom working alone in favour of more active tuition in other groupings;

- offer opportunities for pair work/buddying.

If you want to find out more

Further details on the research study findings

Brooks, G., Burton, M., Cole, P. and Szczerbiński, M. (2007) *Effective Teaching and Learning: Reading.* London: NRDC.

Integrated activities to increase study time

Cooney, T. (2005) 'Good practice: Literacy activities using a variety of texts', *Research and Practice in Adult Literacy (RaPAL) Journal*, Vol. 56, pp. 8–10. (Her suggestions for using 'Jamaica Inn' could be adapted to other stories and plays.)

Issues concerning coercion

O'Grady, A. and Atkin, C. (2005) 'Forced to learn or choosing to learn: Challenges and concerns for non-voluntary adult basic skills learners', *RaPAL Journal*, Vol. 58, pp. 38–43. (Essential reading for providers with non-voluntary learners.)

2 | What can other research tell us about reading?

Introduction

This section looks at useful approaches mentioned in research which don't seem to be used in the adult literacy classroom as often as might be expected. We appreciate that there are reasons for their absence. Target-focused practices, especially the concept of 'teaching to the test' can limit the approaches used. And this, in its turn, helps to reinforce a reluctance to 'take risks', or provide challenges, sometimes expressed as an unwillingness to upset the fragile self-esteem of some learners. One teacher, after successfully trialling oral reading fluency, a strategy she had tended not to use in the past for fear of embarrassing her learners, urged other teachers to: 'Try different methods – even those types of activities you may have avoided in the past.'

Oral reading fluency

By this we mean reading aloud to one or more people.

> *Fluent reading is rapid, accurate and expressive reading, with the momentum unbroken by the need to decode.*

Practice in this, rather than just being a meaningless 'exercise', has been shown to assist reading comprehension and improve confidence. Teachers in England are often reluctant to put their learners under this sort of pressure but research from North America (Kruidenier, 2002) supports incorporating this into normal classroom practice. Indeed it is widely used there both in schools and in adult education.

So that we could have a closer look at this strategy, small-scale trials of oral reading fluency were carried out by NRDC in a selection of adult literacy classes in England between September and December 2006. Only one of the six teachers in the trial had previously used this method much; the others had used it only occasionally, on the grounds that adults might feel too embarrassed to read aloud and that it had school connotations. The teachers tried out various methods and materials with their learners, and they, and 33 of the learners who took part (covering a wide range of ages and levels) gave their evaluations of the project.

"Fluent reading is rapid, accurate and expressive reading, with the momentum unbroken by the need to decode"

The results were very encouraging and suggest that this technique is popular with both teachers and learners. Because this is current research we shall report on it here in some detail. (A fuller account will be available in a forthcoming NRDC report.)

There is a variety of ways of incorporating reading fluency in the classroom. Some helpful guidance can be found in Chapter 5 of McShane (2005). Whatever methods are used, however, the teachers found the following absolutely crucial:

- 'Be open and honest' with your learners; explain and negotiate with them so they understand and feel in control of the process and have the opportunity to voice any concerns.

- Be prepared to adapt any method to suit particular learners, 'not just follow instructions slavishly'.

- Take care in selecting suitable reading materials – those of appropriate level and which are capable of engaging and sustaining interest.

"Be prepared to adapt any method to suit particular learners."

Some methods that can be used to encourage oral reading fluency

Paired reading

The learner reads with a teacher/assistant or another learner at a higher level. They start reading the text together until the learner signals that s/he is happy to read alone. This can increase the amount of pair work in class, already shown to be helpful (p. 4). For a full account of this technique see

http://www.dundee.ac.uk/fedsoc/research/projects/trwresources/.

Choral reading

A group version of the above. It takes pressure off the individual learner but there can be problems if people read at different speeds. An enlarged text, perhaps on an OHP, with a pointer, might resolve that difficulty. Individual learners can signal that they wish to read alone; if they falter, the agreement (negotiated beforehand) is that everyone else will then join back in.

Repeated reading

The same passage is read again and again over the course of a few weeks so that faultless fluency is achieved.

Modelled (echo) reading

Here the teacher reads aloud first and the learner repeats. It is important not to read too long a chunk out – no more than a phrase or short sentence at a time.

Performance reading

Preparing for a 'performance' works particularly well with a play script, with learners taking the individual parts (and the teacher perhaps reading the stage directions). Reminding learners that professional actors don't always get it right can provide reassurance.

"Reminding learners that professional actors don't always get it right can provide reassurance."

Here it is worth mentioning shared reading of texts (for more information see p. 29). The research which informed the National Literacy Strategy (now part of the Primary National Strategy) suggests that an enlarged text read aloud as part of a shared reading activity is more effective than 'round-robin' reading, in terms of fluency, vocabulary acquisition and comprehension (Beard, 2000, p. 36).

Some suggestions for materials to use to encourage reading fluency

Film, TV and play scripts

Plays can be obtained free (often with supporting teaching packs) from theatres. An excellent integrated activity might involve a visit to a local theatre to see a production of the play. It is possible to download TV scripts (for example from soaps such as *EastEnders*) and film scripts from websites such as **http://www.scriptcrawler.net** and **http://www.script-o-rama.com**. There are also short, simple plays available in the Livewire series.

Newspaper articles (p. 32) and **readers** are also good for class discussion. The well-known *Quick Reads*. Other suitable books can be found through First Choice Books (**http://www.firstchoicebooks.org.uk**) and for easier books aimed at beginner readers see New Leaf: **http://www.newleafbooks.org.uk** (the successors to Gatehouse). Graded EFL/ESOL readers can also provide useful reading material for native speakers of English.

Audio books

(To accompany texts, such as New Leaf, and Clipper Emergent Reader Programme – **http://www.wfhowes.co.uk/cerp** – with Quick Reads.) For general information about suitable reading and audio materials see **http://www.vitallink.org.uk**. Recordings provide possibilities for variations on modelled reading and paired reading (and see 'Readalong' in Section 3 for more information).

Learners' own writing

This would provide a familiar text and also reinforce the language experience approach (p. 14).

> **"Peer correction and support were regarded as a particularly effective and valuable outcome."**

The teachers' evaluations of the reading fluency project were very positive, with all six intending to continue to use the strategy regularly. They unanimously considered that enjoyment and engagement in class, confidence, and ability to work independently had improved, and all but one thought it had also improved comprehension. Peer correction and support were regarded as a particularly effective and valuable outcome. It was judged to be suitable for a surprisingly wide range of ages and levels of learners and was a good way of identifying 'hidden problems' which were not apparent if a learner read only silently.

All but five of the 33 learners said they would like to continue with reading aloud in class. Most reported that they felt more confident now about reading aloud. And interestingly, despite the teachers imagining that a one-to-one situation would be less threatening, more than half the learners themselves did not seem to find reading to a group more of a problem than reading to one person.

It would be misleading to suggest that no problems arose, but awareness of and sensitivity to learner needs could obviate some of these. In one case reading aloud uncovered a learner's childhood traumas. The class were reading a play based on Harper Lee's *To Kill a Mockingbird*, to tie in with a visit they made to a local production. The learner, a middle-aged woman, L1, wrote a moving piece about the experience of reading a part aloud, to which she gave a very apt title. Excerpts are given (with her permission) below:

To Kill a Gremlin

I enjoyed the play, it was thought provoking and sad.... . I was unsure if I could read out loud in the classroom. This was only my second time in the class, could I do this, my stomach churned.... . The three just looked at me expectantly. I said ok and picked a small part, I was so frightened. I can't explain how I felt. We read the piece and I didn't look at their faces because it might have shown their reactions.... It just seemed to be getting more frightening each week.... I told our tutor I did not like reading it week after week, I didn't go into details of why I didn't like reading it. Last week we went into a different room to read. I found this easier ... after the reading we talked about the piece and how we felt about reading. It was as if a flood door opened, all my gremlins of school came pouring out. The times I had had a ruler rapped over my knuckles and blackboard rubbers thrown at me because of not understanding or not being able to do the task....The panic I used to feel....The class was sympathetic and encouraging but I found I was really drained.

An observation of this class was carried out the following week. This learner, obviously still in some distress, was given support and encouragement and managed to keep going with a fluent and expressive reading of her part. Afterwards she seemed very proud of her achievement and was 'on a high' for a long time afterwards! (This is an example of risk-taking justified, although the teacher was the first to acknowledge that this learner could have walked out of the door forever.)

It has been suggested that reading aloud is an activity that is hardly ever done by adults. Is this true? Take a minute to think about occasions when you, or others you know, have read something aloud.

Reciprocal teaching

Sometimes known as 'cooperative learning' or 'peer tutoring', reciprocal teaching has been extensively researched in the USA. The starting point is the modelling by the teacher of the strategy being taught and then supporting the learners until they are able to take over the roles of tutor and student and support each other. The main research on this (Palinscar and Brown, 1984) involved the teaching of four specific comprehension-fostering strategies (see pp. 16–17 for more on comprehension), so, for example, one learner might formulate questions for the other learner to answer. The scope for using this could be extended beyond comprehension strategies; it is also another good opportunity for engaging in pair work (p. 8).

Phonics

This topic – much in the news after the Rose Review and the promotion of phonics teaching in schools – tends to arouse very strong feelings. Phonics does get a brief mention in the Core Curriculum (Entry 1, Writing, p. 107). Many adult literacy teachers, however, reject it outright for their learners, especially if the learners' previous experience of phonics was less than positive. But the mounting evidence for the effectiveness of systematic phonics teaching compared with unsystematic or no phonics in initial teaching challenges this view. This does not mean that phonics is the only word identification strategy, but it is a logical starting point for learners whose word identification strategies are weak. Just because a person has reached adulthood, it cannot be assumed that the principles of letter-sound correspondences have been fully grasped along the way. They are not self-evident. One of our consultant teachers, who teaches phonics, reports her learners' realisation of quite basic notions:

> When I've seen words with <igh> in, I've not been able to work them out. Now I know ... that there's only one sound.

(This, incidentally, is a much more helpful way of putting it than talking about 'silent letters'.) Why withhold such vital and empowering information, which could help learners become independent readers?

In the research study we didn't see phonics used very often and when it was, it was generally done on the spur of the moment and was sometimes rather misleading: for example, to say that when you have two vowels together as in the digraph <ea>, the first vowel is the sound you hear might be true of <eat>, <bead>, etc. but there are so many exceptions that as a 'rule' it is not very helpful.

Take a moment to think about other words with <ea> and see what other sounds <ea> can represent. What other examples of oversimplified 'rules' of letter–sound correspondences can you think of? How could these be explored with your learners?

The many 'exceptions' in English are often used to justify the case against phonics but these have been exaggerated. Even 'tricky' common words such as <one>, <two>, <said>, etc. (Dolch List stalwarts) are not totally lacking in sound 'clues'. There is a group of six letters (graphemes) which have relatively stable sound (phoneme) correspondences, <s> <a> <t> <n> <i> <p> – 'satnip' – and form the starting point for school phonics courses such as THRASS (see **http://www.thrass.co.uk**). Our phonics teacher, Janet Whitfield, adapted this system for her adults, changing the illustrations to ones more appropriate for adults. She also recommends phonics tuition for dealing with 'pockets of missing information' which may be unexpected in a learner, who is, say, at Entry 3 and appears competent in reading familiar texts.

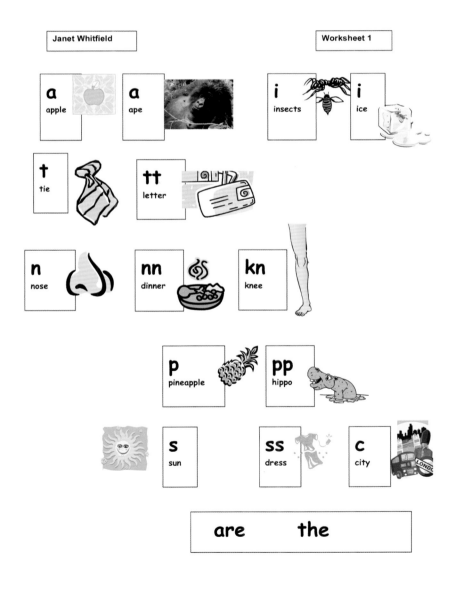

13

One of Janet's worksheets was reproduced on the previous page. Note that a couple of social sight words are also included: 'are' and 'the'. Her main adaptation here, apart from ensuring that the illustrations were appropriate, was to introduce long 'a' and 'i' – which usually feature later in phonics schemes – along with the short versions of these vowels. This was done after consultation with her learners, who found it less confusing to be taught both from the start. It also demonstrates the generally good practice of not following schemes too rigidly and remaining flexible and responsive to the needs of individual learners.

Share the correct terms such as graphemes, phonemes, digraphs and diphthongs with your learners – parents of primary school children may already be familiar with these through the National Literacy Strategy. Knowing the accurate language to talk about language (metalanguage) is crucial. And be sure about the distinction between phonemes and graphemes – easily confused in explanations to learners such as 'vowels saying their names'.

There are many introductory textbooks on the phonetics of English available (see 'If you want to find out more' at the end of this section). There are also websites which offer phonics instruction (mainly in initial literacy); Chapter 4 of McShane (2005) describes phonics from an adult perspective. Other phonics systems that are used for adults in England, apart from THRASS, include the highly structured Toe by Toe (in widespread use in the prison service and for young offenders: **http://www.toe-by-toe.co.uk**) and Sounds~Write (**http://www.sounds-write.co.uk**). For a useful overview of the debates around phonics and suggested materials you could have a look at **http://www.focusonphonics.co.uk**.

Language experience

This is a way of teaching and learning which involves helping the learners to transcribe their own writing and seems to have been at its most popular during the 1970s and 80s but less often used nowadays. It was seen as an inclusive and empowering strategy for emergent writers. Its applications are wider than this, however, and the production of a familiar text can obviously provide the basis for reading activities. Use of a learner's familiar vocabulary and language patterns help to 'bridge that gap between spoken and written English' (Lindsay and Gawn, 2005, p. 38). Language experience is mentioned in the Adult Literacy Core Curriculum as an integrated activity for E1 (pp. 60–1); indeed the strategy is thought of as most appropriate for beginning literacy learners, but it can usefully be used for a wider range of levels. The glossary of The Core Curriculum suggests (p. 139) that the teacher's role is just to produce a written text from what the learner says, but traditionally the activity was much more collaborative. The language experience process can also provide scope for other strategies from oral reading fluency such as paired reading and modelled reading, as the example that follows shows.

An example of language experience in action

With Christine, I would begin with a friendly chat. I would say, 'What have you been doing?' and tell her a bit of what I had been up to. I would then scribe some of what she told me. It would be three or four sentences. I would read it to her and sometimes she would add or change something...I would read it again and get her to join in with the words she could read, and let her take over if she sounded confident. I would make a note of the difficult words to work on later.... Christine would then copy-write the text while I worked with someone else....

I felt it was important that the work should belong to Christine and in the early stages I did not suggest changes of vocabulary of grammar. These came later as I could see her confidence increase. I would then tape the diary entry with the idea that Christine could listen to it and read the text back alongside it at home.'
(From Mace, 2002, p. 188)

Language experience writing is often autobiographical but it need not be. There is, for example, a series of books ('Five Minute Thrillers') in which some are left 'up in the air' to encourage the learners to think about and write alternative endings, a technique described by a consultant teacher as 'very successful' with her learners. Other stories could be stopped before the end to allow for alternative versions to be written and then compared with the actual ending. An article by Celia Drummond (2000) describes the publication of her learners' collaborative writing.

Never forget, of course, that 'a beginner reader is not a beginner thinker'. It was recognition of the validity of student authorship that led to the publication of student writing from the 1970s (e.g. by Gatehouse). Concerns about 'corrections' to a learner's non-standard English can be transformed usefully into a shared critical awareness of the differences between oral and written language. We realise that from the teacher's point of view this can be rather labour-intensive. In the reading study we often saw learners word-processing their handwritten texts – even though it might be more efficient to compose directly on screen – and responding to the computer's checks on spelling and grammar.

"a beginner reader is not a beginner thinker."

> To what extent do you think that this practice can provide a partial replacement for collaboration between teacher and learner?

For a consideration of some of the issues and for ideas for classroom practice, see Wendy Moss's articles (2000, 2005) and especially Jane Mace (2002), one of the champions of this approach.

Explicit comprehension strategies

"what was lacking for many classes was an exploration of different types of questions."

The reading assessment used in the research study was a test of comprehension, and the progress made overall between assessment points was disappointing. Although text-level work observed in classes included answering comprehension questions, these were often in the form of individualised worksheets; what was lacking for many classes was an exploration of different types of questions, coupled with strategies for dealing with them. When we asked learners what they saw as markers of their progress, one learner said that she could now understand 'how they want me to answer certain questions'. This sort of understanding cannot be assumed. Shirley Brice-Heath (1988) notes that, for children, moving from 'what-explanations' to 'reason-explanations' is necessary for the development of reading comprehension. Adults, unlike young children, will generally have essential prior general knowledge to bring to bear on their understanding of a text. But if the conventions of question-answering (whether acquired formally or informally) are poorly understood, then they will be unable to interact effectively with text in order to construct meaning.

Comprehension pre-supposes prior reading skills of decoding and fluency and also knowledge of vocabulary (which does seem to receive attention from teachers – discussion of vocabulary and dictionary use were frequently observed in the classroom). However, strategies of reading comprehension should not be limited to higher-level readers: on the contrary, beginning readers also need to engage in meaningful reading. The use of oral work (the teacher reading aloud or use of recordings) together with class discussion can extend the range of texts that can be tackled.

For an overview of this area, Chapter 7 of McShane (2005) is worth looking at. Several components of comprehension instruction are listed, with some suggestions for ways of implementing them with adults.

Some strategies for teaching comprehension

■ Comprehension monitoring: The teacher demonstrates the thinking processes aloud and gets the learners to practise, e.g. restating short sections, asking themselves questions and/or making notes.

■ Graphic organisers: Diagrams or charts that represent the relationship of ideas and information in the text, e.g. 'spider diagrams' (more familiar as preparation for writing).

■ Story structure to teach awareness of features such as setting, characters, plot, etc.

■ Question answering, not just on matters of fact but crucially teaching readers to make inferences, i.e. to link information from different parts of the text along with their background knowledge. Many learners may not realise that certain questions require answers that are not to be found directly 'in the text'.

■ Question generating, whereby learners ask and answer questions about their reading. This lends itself to the reciprocal teaching approach (p. 11).

■ Summarising, whereby the topic and main ideas are identified.

Obviously these strategies are not mutually exclusive and can be used in various combinations and in different groupings – one-to-one, individual, pairs and whole class. 'Shared reading' (pp. 8, 29) involves group reading of a text with the identification of key features, including 'themes'.

Despite comprehension being central to reading, it is generally an under-researched area, especially for adults. It is always worth remembering that comprehension strategies which are summoned automatically by skilled readers may need to be explained and modelled for less-skilled readers.

Choose a text and in your own reading of it work out how you apply comprehension strategies. How best can you model them for your learners?

Conclusion

We have outlined strategies which seem sound theoretically but are not often used with adults and which would benefit from further research to support using them in the classroom. We're not saying at this stage that they do work, just that they are definitely worth a try. Practitioners can be reluctant to be too innovative although some of the best innovations have of course, stemmed from practice.

"Remember that risk-taking can be very empowering for both teacher and learner"

Ask yourself:

■ If there are any strategies outlined in this section that I avoid for my learners, why?

■ How do you know your reasons are justified? Try discussing them with your learners.

And:

■ Try out some of the strategies outlined in this section as part of your own research.

If you want to find out more

Oral reading fluency

McShane, S. (2005) Chapter 5, 'Fluency development'. At:
> http://www.nifl.gov/partnershipforreading/publications/html/
> mcshane/chapter5.html

Phonetics of English

Familiarity with the phonetics of English is helpful underpinning knowledge for *phonics*. See, for example:

Cruttenden, A. (2001) *Gimson's Pronunciation of English* (6th edn). London: Hodder Arnold. (Useful reference source of phonemes and how they are represented in English spelling.)

Roach, P. (2000) *The Phonetics of English: A Practical Course* (3rd edn). Cambridge University Press. (A clear textbook, with accompanying CDs or cassettes.)

Also see:

McShane, S. (2005) As before – Chapter 4, 'Alphabetics: Phonemic awareness training and phonics instruction'. At: **http://www.nifl.gov/ partnershipforreading/publications/html/mcshane/chapter4.html**

Language experience

Examples of language experience in action:

Drummond, C. (2000) 'Exegesis Book Club: Adult basic education students write books for other students to read' *RaPAL Bulletin*, Vol. 40, pp. 23–6. (Account of classroom activity where learners, with the teacher's help, collaboratively wrote and saw through to publication stories targeted specifically at a readership of adult emergent readers.)

Mace, J. (2002) 'Scribes and authors in adult literacy', in: *The Give and Take of Writing*, pp. 183–197. Leicester: NIACE.

Moss, W. (2000) 'Talk into text: Reflections on the relationship between author and scribe in writing through language experience', *RaPAL Bulletin*, Vol. 40, pp. 12–13.

Moss. W. (2005) 'Theories on the teaching of reading to adults: Some notes', RaPAL Journal, Vol. 56, pp. 24–5.

Explicit comprehension strategies

McShane, S. (2005) As before – Chapter 7, 'Comprehension-strategy instruction'. At **http://www.nifl.gov/partnershipforreading/ publications/html/mcshane/chapter7.html**

Useful websites

Oral reading fluency

Books and audio books: **http://www.firstchoicebooks.org.uk**; **http://www.newleafbooks.org.uk**; **http://www.wfhowes.co.uk/cerp**; **http://www.vitallink.org.uk**

Paired reading: **http://www.dundee.ac.uk/fedsoc/research/projects/trwresources/**

Play and film scripts: **http://www.scriptcrawler.net** and
http://www.script-o-rama.com

Phonics

http://www.focusonphonics.co.uk

http://www.sounds-write.co.uk

http://www.thrass.co.uk

http://www.toe-by-toe.co.uk

3 How can we use professional wisdom in our practice?

By 'professional wisdom' we mean the insights and experience of practitioners.

> Making good decisions about applying research findings also means understanding individual learners, groups and classroom settings so your instruction acknowledges their particular characteristics. The judgement that you've acquired through experience also enters the decision-making process. Together these forms of knowledge may be called professional wisdom (McShane, 2005, Ch 2, p. 4).

Importantly, this also involves reflecting on your own practice as a practitioner. What emerged very strongly in the research study was the fact that teachers appear to have little time or opportunity for reflection; observing in other practitioners' classrooms and analysing what went on proved a helpful way of gaining an overview of different teaching and learning strategies. Attending related conferences helped to put their experience into a wider context. Our practitioner-researchers also mentioned such factors in their personal and professional development as becoming 'more critical of my own teaching and planning', gaining 'insight', and 'extending the boundaries of my self-perceived expertise'.

Throughout the preceding sections there have been points at which you have been asked to stop and consider – and perhaps challenge – what we have written, drawing on your own knowledge and experience. Ideally this would also happen as part of normal professional life, with the opportunity to reflect and share on a regular basis. This section offers a selection of further insights that emerged from meetings and correspondence with our consultation group, arranged under various headings. It was interesting and significant that our practitioner group was always keen to discuss teaching and learning in more general terms than just specific strategies for reading. This very much reflects a view of adult literacy teaching and learning as operating in a context that is wider than a set of classroom-based skills and strategies.

Concern for the learners emerged as paramount for teachers in the research study and it was striking how much the teachers' sense of well-being depended on their learners being happy. In Section 1 we discussed some of the factors about learners that seemed to affect progress but were not within the control of their teachers. To these we can add issues around *health* and *support*. Progress might be slower for learners who have health problems; and not having support at home or at work from family and peers could be detrimental to progress. The following are other (interrelated) issues that can affect the progress learners make.

Confidence

The importance of building confidence and self-esteem for adult literacy learners might seem self-evident:

> 'The self-esteem construct is recognised today to be a major factor in learning outcomes. Research has consistently shown a positive correlation between how people value themselves and the level of their academic attainments' (Lawrence, 2000, p. xviii)

So yes, it is crucial, although as we saw in the research study the confidence-progress relationship is complex and different factors have to be taken into consideration.

Difficulties of 'measuring' growth in confidence

Teachers can be aware of quite subtle changes. When we asked learners about their 'enjoyment' of various literacy activities in the attitudes questionnaire, one of our teachers suggested that, even if she could see a change in a learner, lack of confidence might prevent that learner from admitting to any such enjoyment. Another complexity is the fact that some learners do appear to 'go backwards' with increasing confidence. (The types of mistakes made in the final assessments in the research study suggest this, as though increasing confidence may have made them more likely to tackle harder questions but get them wrong.)

Concepts of failure and success

These are seen as lying at the heart of learner confidence. That 'classic' book by Good and Holmes, *How's it Going? An Alternative to Testing Students in Adult Literacy*, despite, as the title suggests, arguing for more flexible measures of progress to be negotiated with the learner, actually warns against trying to prevent learners from experiencing failure (e.g. by not giving them 'tests' they might fail). This is because in the real world, 'failure will come. So protecting students in this way is likely to slow down their rate of learning in the long run' (Good and Holmes, 1982, p. 3). Strategies for facing challenges and dealing with failure are also empowering. Errors and mistakes should actually be welcomed.

An example of building positively on a learner's mistake from the research study:

> A learner is reading out an account of a woman giving birth to a very light baby, and gives the baby's weight as '11 lbs'. After checking, the teacher explains that the she has confused 1 with l and so misread 1lb as 11lb. The teacher asks the class where they think lb comes from; prompts by mentioning star signs. Another learner says 'Libra' and the teacher praises, asking what the symbol for Libra is. The learner says 'scales' and is praised. The teacher writes 'Libra' on the board and draws some scales, telling the learners that Libra is old language for weighing.

Drawbacks of 'playing safe'

Often teachers regard their role as protecting their learners from failure by building successful outcomes into each lesson. This is fine as far as it goes, but not if it stops teachers taking any risks or setting any challenges. One of the observed teachers from the reading study was reluctant to 'let' a particular learner take the reading assessment, but once she had been persuaded to let him have a go, she realised that she had been over-protective and by letting him be challenged, enabled him to make huge strides. Treating learners too cautiously and making too many allowances for them, as though they are so very different from the general population, is actually buying into an unacceptable deficit model.

Teachers make mistakes too!

Mistakes on the part of the teacher should also be acknowledged; it is liberating for learners to know that 'professionals' don't always get it right!

Learners also have knowledge

Building confidence can often involve building on what learners already know, e.g. that there are social sight signs they are able to read, or the names of television programmes that can be identified from a newspaper (and see 'Shared reading', p. 29).

"it is liberating for learners to know that 'professionals' don't always get it right!"

Example from research study of a learner's knowledge:

> When the fieldworker gave the reading assessment (a test of comprehension based on a simulated magazine with questions) to a particular class, she was told by the teacher that learner K could read 'absolutely nothing' and it would be a 'waste of time' trying to include him in the assessment. When she showed the magazine to K, he shook his head immediately and said he couldn't – and wouldn't – do it. Afterwards, before leaving that class she again gave K the magazine to look at and found that he was actually able to pick out and read several individual words, including 'TV', 'DIY', 'garden' and 'films'. He then told her that he was able to find out what was on TV by picking out the information from TV magazines.

It is also worth demonstrating that learners' judgements and views about reading and books are valid.

> A learner (working towards Level 2) loved the novels of Virginia Andrews and was encouraged by her teacher to do a research project on her. In the process she discovered various articles, uniformly scathing in their criticism of the writer's private life and her literary ability. After initial surprise and disappointment, this learner concluded that 'the novelist's books are brilliant ... her private life is her business and does not influence the way I feel about her books.'

Engagement

In the research study the examples of good teaching practice that were singled out by our practitioner-researchers were often the ones where there was felt to be enthusiasm and engagement on the part of the learners.

Learners' interests and hobbies

Engaging learners may be as simple as responding to their particular interests. In a class in the research study, for example, an interest in art was related to a word-search with colour names, reading about Van Gogh, followed by a library visit for further art research.

Humour

Humour was also identified as an important ingredient, with praise for teachers who made sessions 'fun'. One teacher reports successfully harnessing a learner's 'sense of fun' by using cartoons, and modelling 'dramatic readings and exaggeration', although this approach might not be appropriate for some learners. 'Social sight' signs can also incorporate humour.

WAY OUT →
← EXIT

Above all, humour is a useful weapon to combat expectations that learning will not be enjoyable and to lay to rest the ghosts of bad school experiences.

Democracy

Having learners as 'democratic partners' in the learning process is of fundamental importance. Our consultant teachers often reminded us that learners should not be people who have activities and strategies imposed on them in the classroom. This approach invokes Freire and his critique of the banking concept of education:

> Knowledge is a gift bestowed by those who consider themselves knowledgeable upon those whom they consider to know nothing. (Freire, 1996, p. 53)

> I am big on democratic understanding. I think it is fundamental that students understand where we are coming from, why we are doing the things we do, exactly how each method works and exactly what it is aimed at achieving. (Consultant teacher)

Collaboration

Awareness on the part of the learners of the processes that go on in teaching and learning reading also extends to processes of assessment and a shared understanding of the strategies that might enable further progress.

We don't impose strategies on learners: we discuss and test them out with learners, resulting in joint evaluation. (Consultant teacher)

Learners can be encouraged to share with each other the strategies which work (or don't) for them.

On learners sharing strategies with each other:

'A powerful' resource which 'led to learners feeling empowered and in greater control of the reading process.' (Consultant teacher)

Feeling in control in this way helps learners take responsibility for their own learning, whether in terms of making the time to read a page of a book at home or even just appreciating the value of turning up at class each week.

Choice and freedom

Choice and freedom are also aspects of being in control. Learners can be encouraged, e.g. to work in pairs or to read aloud in class, but must also be free not to. One teacher offered freedom to choose what and whether to read: a selection of books was available on a table and she saw her role as facilitating reading rather than 'pushing' it. This had a good outcome: a fifty-year-old learner (L1) ended up reading a book for the very first time (an ESOL-adapted Penguin classic) and is now 'a reader'.

Indeed there must be freedom even to 'opt out' of wider and generally accepted values about reading. This entails a measure of open-mindedness on the part of the teacher.

An open mind

"Some learners might be intimidated by libraries and avoid books but be happy to read magazines."

It is easy to take certain concepts for granted. For example, reading for pleasure is regarded as something unquestionably good and there are certainly outstanding materials available such as Quick Reads, with guidance on supporting activities and web-based ideas (**http://www.quickreadsideas.org.uk**) and on the value of public libraries (**http://www.vitallink.org.uk**). However, it has been pointed out by our consultant teachers that care is sometimes needed with this concept. It is not always appropriate – it may be enough for some learners that they read 'for interest', or even just 'well enough'. If reading for pleasure is held out as something to aspire to, then people may feel they have failed if they don't achieve this. Some learners might be intimidated by libraries and avoid books but be happy to read magazines. The same applies to having 'educational' posters promoting reading up in the classroom – they can be intimidating for some learners.

Different assumptions

Remember that learners may not share the same assumptions about what reading means and what is involved. An example of this was where a learner claimed she didn't read anything but it turned out she did a Bible reading in church every Sunday! Make no prior assumptions about higher-level readers' knowledge – there may be surprising gaps; or about the abilities of beginner readers – they may know more than you, or they, realise, as demonstrated in the 'Confidence' section by the research study example on learner's knowledge (p. 22). Learner K's refusal to engage with text in class had misled the teacher into seriously underestimating his ability.

Take nothing for granted

Not even the most 'basic' notions.

I didn't know that when the same two letters come together in a word (e.g. double consonant in dinner) there's only one sound. If I'd have known that it would have helped me a lot. (Entry-level learner)

And as we found when developing oral reading fluency (p. 7), when you ask learners to read aloud it can highlight difficulties that you are unaware of (especially with apparently more 'able' readers) if they only read silently in class.

Try and see things from the learners' point of view

Of course, unpicking what is going on takes time. And what learners perceive as real markers of their progress may be quite individual and idiosyncratic: learners (and their teachers) have told us many different stories which demonstrate real pride in their achievements – for example, about reading that first book, writing the first letter ever to a brother, reading to grandchildren, having a letter published in a newspaper, or even just plucking up courage to enquire about classes.

Just as these factors arose out of discussions with teachers and learners there may be other factors that you will want to add from your own experience. What else do you regard as important for your learners if they are to make progress?

Classroom management

Many of the teachers we spoke to bemoaned the target-driven culture, the excessive paperwork and the lack of time to spend with individual learners, in order to assess their needs and teach accordingly. It was felt that far more time should be made available for finding out exactly what reading your learners wanted to be able to do. At the same time, however, the value for some learners of obtaining a qualification shouldn't be underestimated.

Although aspects of the system are outside the control of teachers, what you can take ownership of is the organisation of grouping and structure of the lesson.

Learners should not work on their own for too long

We have already seen how important this (p. 4) but finding appropriate activities for whole-class work can be difficult with groups of learners of different ages and abilities. In the oral reading fluency project, we found that play reading helped to draw together disparate groups of learners and other suggestions are made elsewhere in this guide.

Using volunteers

Increasing the amount of one-to-one work to increase time on task would require higher staffing levels, although where volunteers and assistants are available they are frequently paired one-to-one with the weaker learners in the class. This may not always be the wisest combination, as it actually requires more expertise to help a beginner reader than a more able one. We have seen inexperienced assistants make the mistake, when listening to reading, of jumping in too quickly to 'help', before the learner has had a chance to apply decoding strategies.

"constant use of one-to-one tuition can be too intensive for the learner."

Working almost exclusively with the volunteer also has the tendency to single those learners out, setting them apart from the more able members of the group. (Consultant teacher)

In general, constant use of one-to-one tuition can be too intensive for the learner and, worse, can result in dependency and disempowerment, if the learner starts to believe that s/he is unable to work without this support.

Communicate your lesson plan

Explaining what you intend to do in a lesson and why is always good practice: this can be incorporated into a whole-class opening section to discuss the aims for the session (linking it to previous work), with a similar closing session to summarise what has been achieved. We know that this can be difficult to achieve when learners arrive and leave at different times but it is worth persevering with. It is motivating and empowering for learners to have a clear plan of what you and they are trying to achieve.

Strategies and materials

Teaching methods should empower the learners and lead ultimately to independent learning. And they must always be appropriate for the particular learners – always be prepared to adapt methods. We were told about one inexperienced assistant who was trying to help a learner decode words by cutting them in half for him, a strategy which bore no relation to what that learner needed. Our practitioners suggested many effective methods and materials used by them, or observed in action, which you can try out or adapt for your own context.

"– always be prepared to adapt methods."

Shared reading

This can work with or without reading aloud. Various texts can be used, both fiction and non-fiction (incident report in a care home, sets of instructions, etc.). It is an inclusive group activity in which the tutor begins by activating prior knowledge of the learners. They are encouraged (with questioning) to contribute what they already know about the content and the type of text (purpose?, audience?, features of grammar/punctuation?, etc.). After discussing the text as a whole group, the class can be supported in smaller groups to share and record their ideas and experience about the topic. From there the teacher can differentiate the work of individuals or groups with follow-on activities at text, sentence or word level (see http://www.literacytrust.org.uk/Pubs/shared.html).

'Readalong'

Learners are given cassettes/CDs with recordings of material which the tutor has recorded – stories, instructions, short news items, etc. – to listen to as they read. Be aware that some commercially produced audio books may go too fast for emergent readers, or omit chunks of text. 'Home-made' recordings can avoid these pitfalls. However, CDs from New Leaf (www.newleafbooks.org.uk) to accompany their books seem well designed for emergent readers as they offer slower reading versions as well as listening speed ones. These can be offered as 'homework' for the learner to listen to while reading the text. The idea is to give reluctant readers more practice at reading, either aloud, or for silent reading practice. (Hugo Kerr)

'Exploded text'

A method of teaching autonomous self-correction of written work (could be used in conjunction with a language experience approach). Each sentence in turn is read aloud by the learner, who then asks him/herself questions such as 'Do I like this sentence? Does it sound right? Does it say what I want it to say?', etc., before going on to examine it for details of spelling and punctuation. (Hugo Kerr)

'Real world flash'

A method of learning social sight vocabulary, using photos of real signs. Each slide is shown briefly (less than a second), e.g. CAR PARK, followed by a blank screen which remains until the group has called out 'car park'. The signs can grow in length and complexity as the 'slide show' proceeds. It is not only entertaining for the learners but seems to produce results (Kerr, 2005). This technique can be extended, for example, to words from the Dolch List.

> The ideas above have arisen out of first-hand experience in the classroom. Think about whether you have developed (or have an idea for) an effective strategy that is innovative in some way. Try explaining it or writing about it in enough detail for another practitioner to take away to use.

Reading materials for learners should be:

- appropriate for the learner's reading level and interests. If you can get this right, then a reluctant reader can turn into an enthusiastic one;
- 'real' in the sense of relating to real life. Decontextualised exercises are limited and limiting. Encouraging learners to bring in their own materials is one way to bring 'realia' into the classroom. Judging by the research study, worksheets are alive and well but excessive use of them 'without rhyme or reason' is ill-advised.

Realia

Example of realia from the research study:

> Learner M, working one-to-one with volunteer tutor N, has brought notes from a church meeting she attended, the agenda and some leaflets about the venue. N tells me (the observer) that she was unable to attend that meeting herself, so M is going to tell her about it, while writing up her notes into a report. M tells N about the Centre where the meeting was held, showing her leaflets and maps.

As another example of easily obtainable realia, newspapers, including the Metro, and other free local papers, can be used in many different ways (also mentioned in connection with homework, p. 2, and oral reading fluency, p. 7). Local and national interest articles can lend themselves particularly well to class discussion with a range of learners, and are another way of bringing together quite heterogeneous groups.

Creativity with newspapers

One consultant teacher mentions doing 'very creative work' from newspapers whereby learners were asked to project themselves into the newspaper story and become one of the characters involved. They then wrote about 'the "real" story behind the news', talking about their own feelings and attitudes.

The internet

The most frequently used Internet materials in the classroom are from dedicated websites such as **http://www.bbc.co.uk/skillswise** and **http://www.talent.ac.uk**, but we have also seen and like the inventive use of other sites such as the BBC Weather site, Egyptology sites for a project on hieroglyphics and websites on local tourist attractions. A fascinating new website on surnames offers scope for combining a name search with geography: see **http://www.spatial-literacy.org/ UCLnames**.

A note on colours and fonts

Coloured overlays, more usually associated with dyslexia, can be helpful for some students. Similarly a choice of different computer screen colours can be used effectively. We saw a variety of colours in use, although paler colours would be better generally than the deep purple screen that one learner (from the research study) – exercising freedom of choice – seemed happy with! Experimenting with different fonts, spacing and sizes of print can also be helpful for learners.

Reducing the wealth of information and experience we collected to a set of headings and bullet points does not do justice to it. Nor is this an exhaustive list.

We hope that there are other factors, strategies and resources that occur to you. Try and find ways of sharing and reflecting on them with colleagues.

If you want to find out more

Benefits of reading aloud while listening

Britten, G. (2005) 'Write to Read: A reading intervention strategy', *RaPAL Journal*, Vol. 56, pp.16–18. (An account of group reading while following texts read aloud.)

On learning social sight vocabulary

Kerr, H. (2004) 'Real World Flash: A technique described and feedback sought', *RaPAL Journal*, Vol. 55, p. 10.

For general ideas and resources

Basic Skills Agency, *The Starter Pack.* (Teaching ideas and tips with a CD-ROM). See: **http://publications.basic–skills.co.uk**

The DfES Access for All website on the reading process, with links to the Adult Core Curriculum. See: **http://www.dfes.gov.uk/curriculum_literacy/tree/reading/access**

The RaPAL (Research and Practice in Adult Literacy) journals, published three times a year, have practical teaching ideas as well as research-based articles: **http://www.literacy.lancs.ac.uk/rapal/**. Issue 51 from 2003 has a large section with members' views on useful references for professional development.

The resources menus produced by Tribal CTAD are available on CD-ROM. They aim to point providers towards suitable *Skills for Life* resources. See: **http://www.ctad.co.uk**

Other useful websites

Guidance on supporting activities and web-based ideas for Quick Reads: **http://www.quickreadsideas.org.uk**

Value of public libraries: **http://www.vitallink.org.uk**

Shared reading: **http://www.literacytrust.org.uk/Pubs/shared.html**

Audio books for beginner readers: **http://www.newleafbooks.org.uk**

Sources of web-based materials and ideas: **http://www.bbc.co.uk/skillswise; http://www.talent.ac.uk; http://www.spatial–literacy.org/UCLnames**

4 What next?

Further research

Throughout this guide we have outlined some of the latest research on teaching reading, offered suggestions for practice and encouraged debate and reflection on practice. As always with research, as many questions are raised as answered, and the next NRDC projects carried out by the University of Sheffield will focus on oral language fluency and phonics.

We conclude by suggesting some topics for small-scale action research projects which could be undertaken with your classes and/or your colleagues. The immediate benefits might be to you and your learners but can reach beyond. One of the Reading Fluency Project teachers mentioned that her involvement in the project received a positive mention in their latest inspection report and also that she was able to share information on reading fluency with other teachers during a staff development session.

Some of the talking points may already have prompted ideas for projects, and we hope that you may consider trying out some of the approaches outlined in sections 2 and 3. Here are some other ideas:

- Finding out what learners perceive as real markers of their progress. Which is more important to them – gaining a qualification or other milestones?
- Phonics – a survey of teachers' experience of and attitudes to teaching phonics to adults and/or learners' understanding of letter–sound relationships.
- Finding ways for your learners to work in pairs – first of all negotiating, and explaining that they are a resource for each other; trying out different combinations (same levels, different levels) and different approaches, e.g. paired reading, reciprocal teaching, etc.
- Having devised imaginative homework tasks (p. 2), use the feedback from your learners to assess which types of task prove the most popular and effective.

Some key points to remember:

- Take risks by trying out new approaches to teaching reading.

- Find ways of expanding learners' time 'on task'.

- Do not be over-protective of your learners.

- Reflect on and share what you do with colleagues, at meetings, conferences, etc.

- Keep an open mind – take nothing for granted.

- Above all, trust your own judgement.

Your contribution to extending knowledge in the field of adult literacy as a practitioner-researcher is valid and valuable. As one of our consultant teachers memorably wrote of her involvement in the Reading Study,

Although research should inform practice, practice can inform research. The practitioner-researchers embody this symbiosis.

References

Adams, M.J. (1994) *Beginning to Read: Thinking and Learning About Print.* Cambridge, MA: MIT. (Comprehensive review of the debates around reading instruction for children.)

Barton, D. (1994) *Literacy.* Oxford: Blackwell.

Barton, D. and Hamilton, M. (1998) *Local Literacies.* London: Routledge.

Basic Skills Agency (2001) *Adult Literacy Core Curriculum.* London: Basic Skills Agency.

Beard, R. (2000) *National Literacy Strategy: Review of Research and Other Related Evidence.* London: DfEE.

Britten, G. (2005) 'Write to Read: A reading intervention strategy', *RaPAL Journal,* Vol. 56, pp. 16–18.

Brooks, G., Burton, M., Cole, P. and Szczerbinski, M. (2007) *Effective Teaching and Learning: Reading.* London: NRDC.

Brooks, G. *et al.* (2001) *Progress in Adult Literacy: Do Learners Learn?* London: Basic Skills Agency.

Chapman, J.W. and Tunmer, W.E. (2003) 'Reading difficulties, reading-related self-perceptions and strategies for overcoming negative self-beliefs', *Reading and Writing Quarterly,* Vol. 19, pp. 5–24.

Cooney, T. (2005) 'Good practice: Literacy activities using a variety of texts', *RaPAL Journal,* Vol. 56, pp. 8–10.

Cruttenden, A. (2001) *Gimson's Pronunciation of English* (6th edn). London: Edward Arnold.

Drummond, C. (2000) 'Exegesis Book Club: Adult basic education students write books for other students to read', *RaPAL Bulletin,* Vol. 40, pp. 23–6. (Account of classroom activity where learners, with the teacher's help, collaboratively wrote and saw through to publication stories, targeted specifically at a readership of adult emergent readers.)

Freire, P. (1996) *Pedagogy of the Oppressed.* Harmondsworth: Penguin.

Galbraith, A. and Alexander, J. (2005) 'Literacy, self-esteem and locus of control', *Support for Learning*, Vol. 20, No. 1.

Good, M. and Holmes, J. (1982) *How's it Going? An Alternative to Testing Students in Adult Literacy*. ALBSU.

Heath, S.B. (1988) 'What no bedtime story means: Narrative skills at home and school', in N. Mercer (ed.) *Language and Literacy from an Educational Perspective, Vol II*. Milton Keynes: Open University Press.

Holme, R. (2004) *Literacy: An Introduction*. Edinburgh: Edinburgh University Press.

Kerr, H. (2004) 'Real World Flash: A technique described and feedback sought', *RaPAL Journal*, Vol. 55, p. 10.

Kruidenier, J. (2002) *Research-based Principles for Adult Basic Education Reading Instruction*. Portsmouth, NH: National Institute for Literacy.

Lawrence, D. (2000) *Building Self-Esteem with Adult Learners*. London: Paul Chapman Publishing Ltd.

LDA (n.d) *Five Minute Thrillers*. LDA. See: **http://www.ldalearning.com**

Lindsay, A. and Gawn, J. (2005) *Developing Literacy Skills: Supporting Achievement*. Leicester: NIACE. (Brief but helpful overview of a variety of issues and strategies.)

Mace. J. (1995) *Literacy, Language and Community Publishing: Essays in Adult Education*. Clevedon: Multilingual Matters.

Mace, J. (2002) 'Scribes and authors in Adult Literacy', Chapter 9, *The Give and Take of Writing*, pp. 183–97. Leicester: NIACE.

McShane, S. (2005) *Applying Research in Reading Instruction for Adults. First Steps for Teachers*. Washington, DC: National Institute for Literacy. (Can be downloaded from **http://www.nifl.gov/partnershipforreading/publications/html/mcshane/index** where there are links to all the chapters. Useful American work.)

Moss, W. (2000) 'Talk into Text: Reflections on the relationship between author and scribe in writing through language experience', *RaPAL Bulletin*, Vol. 40, pp. 12–13.

Moss. W. (2005) 'Theories on the teaching of reading to adults: some notes', *RaPAL Journal*, Vol. 56, pp. 24–5.

O'Grady, A. and Atkin, C. (2005) 'Forced to learn or choosing to learn: Challenges and concerns for non-voluntary adult basic skills learners', *RaPAL Journal*, Vol. 58, pp. 38–43.

Palinscar, A.S. and Brown, A.L. (1984) 'Reciprocal teaching of comprehension-fostering and comprehension-monitoring activities', *Cognition and Instruction* Vols 1 and 2, pp. 117–72.

Reder, S. (2005) 'Literacy and the life course', *Reflect* (magazine of NRDC), no. 2 (September), pp. 16–17.

Roach, P. (2000) *The Phonetics of English: A Practical Course* (3rd edn). Cambridge: Cambridge University Press.

Street, B. (1984) *Literacy in Theory and Practice*. Cambridge: Cambridge University Press.

Street, B. (2005) 'Understanding and defining literacy', paper commissioned for the *Education for All Global Monitoring Report 2006, Literacy for Life*.

Stubbs, M. (1981) *Language and Literacy*. London: Routledge & Kegan Paul.